MW00950626

Cageless

By Josh "Mode" Ford

This publication contains the opinions and ideas of its author. It is intended to provide helpful and informative material on the subjects addressed in the publication. The author and publisher specifically disclaim all responsibility for any liability, loss, or risk, personal or otherwise, that is incurred as a consequence, directly or indirectly of the use or application of any of the contents of this book.

Copyright © 2017 by Josh Ford. All rights reserved. No part of this book may be modified, reproduced, or transmitted in any form or by any means, electronic or mechanical, including emailing, photocopying, recording, or otherwise without the prior written permission of the publisher.

Jordan Jada Journey

Another book dedication that isn't about you, huh? Well not this time. This book right here... This book is for you. Yes, you reading this right now. This book is dedicated to you and everyone who has ever felt caged and felt as if you weren't good enough. Continue to pursue your dreams and fulfill your purpose. We always seem to fall short but we get up. Let go of the things that limit you!

The Panther

His vision, from the constantly passing bars,

has grown so weary that it cannot hold

anything else. It seems to him there are

a thousand bars; and behind the bars, no world.

As he paces in cramped circles, over and over,

the movement of his powerful soft strides

is like a ritual dance around a center

in which a mighty will stands paralyzed.

Only at times, the curtain of the pupils

lifts, quietly. An image enters in,

rushes down through the tensed, arrested muscles,

plunges into the heart and is gone.

~Rainer Maria Rilke

Contents

Chapter 10 - Walk the Walk

Introduction

We huddled up. Our football team, the University of Colorado Buffaloes, needed a big play. As a freshman, scrimmages were always my time to shine and contend. This scrimmage was going great and I was competing. We always strived and pushed non-stop at CU. Our motto was, "The pride and tradition of the Colorado Buffaloes will not be entrusted to the timid or the weak."

We were in the huddle beat up. It was our "Offense vs. Defense competition." The defense had been killing us all day. Nonetheless it all came down to this next play. The situation is simple: we need a first down. We are backed up on our goal line and have seven yards to get it. This is the final play.

It's all about who wants it more, our offense or the defense. I stand in the backfield scanning the defense, pre-snap reading their formation.

We all huddle up and glance over to the sideline at Coach to get the play call. He signals in "97 Oakland." All the plays in football are coded. The "9" in 97 meant it was a two-back set. The "7" meant the aiming point and the "O" in Oakland meant the run was going to the outside.

Instantly, it's about to go down! It's about to get wild. Oakland is an outside handoff, as the running back. If I don't make this play, we lose. I must make a play when my number is called.

We all break the huddle and run to the line. Jordan, our QB goes through his cadence and the ball is snapped, getting an amazing push from the offensive line.

I take the handoff, press the line and I hit the hole with ambition. Maneuvering through the linebackers, stiff-arming defenders, I break loose down the sideline, sprinting towards the end zone, seeing nothing but daylight, hearing nothing but my pads ruffling and the wind blowing. It's a huge gain thus far.

The safety tackles me from behind. Nonetheless, of the seven yards I needed, I picked up fifty-two yards on an explosive play. The offense was hyped. We won the competition and we were ecstatic! It was just what the team needed.

I ran over to the sideline, getting daps and handshakes from my teammates. Chest bumps and hi fives all over the offense.

I couldn't wait to see the look on Coach's face. I see him from a distance and know he is ready to dap up and celebrate.

As we get closer to each other, I'm grinning from ear to ear.I look at Coach. He has this irate look in his eye. I saw no flags and there were no penalties. I don't know what's wrong. I know he's coming to show love, though.

Coach walks up to me. He asks, "Why didn't you score?"

Uhh... didn't know what to say. Coach repeated, "Why didn't you score!!?"

I didn't have an answer.

Coach shouted, "Score next time!!" and walked away.

I was irked. I just broke a long run down the sidelines. Why is Coach upset? Though the offense won and my guys were happy, I was still processing what Coach said. I was confused all night.

I even started taking it personally, questioning myself. Was my run not good enough?

Eventually, I just slept on it. Besides, we had team workouts early in the morning at 5 am, so I went to bed early.

The next morning I woke up energized and ready to go before the sun rose. I hadn't forgotten about the previous day, but I was ready to lift weights.

The weight room was my meditation sanctuary. A lot of guys on my team skipped or slacked off in team workouts. But I used it as an opportunity to get better, to get strong and develop. It's where I would push myself daily and destroy myself, so to speak, so nobody could destroy me.

I walk into the weight room and the first person I see is Coach on the treadmill, getting in his early morning workout. I immediately went into defense mode, ready to shield anything he has to say.

Coach looked at me and said, "Good morning, 42. How you doing?" (Coach called every player by their jersey number.)

Confused, I wanted to say, "Man do you not remember yesterday?" but instead, I muttered, "Morning, Coach. I see you grinding," and continued on to my workout stations. As the morning goes on, Coach spots me a couple times and says, "Keep getting strong. It builds confidence."

He also told me to swing by his office after workouts.

Workouts end.

Nervous but eager, I entered his office.

It was a mess, not a dirty, nasty mess but a productive "I have lots of things going on" mess. Coach had so many plays, scripts and other paperwork all over the place.

"What's up, 42? Come in and grab a seat," he said.

Coach had pictures up of all his past ventures. He coached some of the greatest running backs of all time, such as Adrian Peterson, Chester Taylor, Maurice Jones-Drew, Jamal Charles and Chris Brown. He also worked with some of the most influential people in the world, such as Coach Andy Reid. He's so humble, though, that he never mentioned it at all.

He said, "So, how are you? How's school?"

"School's going good, and I'm doing well," I said.

"Good," he replied.

He knew something was on my mind. Coach always treated his players as men. He told me to speak my mind.

I hesitated for a second... I looked him in the eye and asked about yesterday's scrimmage, specifically my long run.

He grinned and said, "Here's the thing, 42, I want you to be the best, and I know the player you can become. I know what you're capable of, 42. The world is full of average players. Average gets you nowhere and I want you to be great."

His words blew me away. I knew he really harvested my potential and always made sure I was on the right track.

However, I had to ask him to explain yesterday.

He told me something that I'll never ever forget. "Good is the enemy of great. Good is what an average person does. I want greatness from my players."

I needed you to make that play and score. But you let the safety tackle you from behind. You have to push yourself!

You started coasting, when you could have sprinted through the end zone.

"Take nothing for granted" he said. "When you have an opportunity to score, go score! Same in life, if you have the opportunity to do something great, do it. You'll never know when the opportunity will present itself again."

"What do I have to do to get better and be great, in school, my life and athletics?" I asked.

"Break out of the cage," Coach said.

I was confused? A cage? What is that, the matrix? I'm not in a cage. He pulled up a picture of a lion in a zoo, in a small cage. He explained to me that the lions were not created to live in zoos or cages. They are active animals.

In the zoo, lions have everything given to them. The zoo staff feeds them; they don't hunt, they even have their mate chosen for them and just lie there all day.

That's not what lions are meant to do. That's not what they were created for. They were not made to live in cages; they were built to roam and hunt. They are very active and need to be free. They weren't made to just walk in circles and play with chew toys like you see in zoos. In fact, I believe the lion can break out of the zoo cage anytime he wants, but that's all he knows.

I was blown away by what Coach had said, how true and real it all was.

He planted a seed of a paradigm change in me. Instantly, this cage of just being average, just going through the motions was malfunctioning.

I began to reflect on all the times I felt caged, times when I knew I could do better and I didn't. I even thought about the cages I was currently inside, the cages that I knew were holding me back.

I'm not fully un-caged; I'm not fully free, although I've broken out of many cages. I'm still developing and breaking free. However, the cages that I have broken from inspired me to write this book and help others get out of their cages.

One cage I broke from is the "nobody makes it from the hood cage" that everybody tried to put on my neighborhood.

Though I grew up in Montbello, Colorado (in Denver) with few opportunities, I was able to achieve a double major and pursue grad school, as well as play football professionally. I did not become an unfortunate, institutionalized statistic.

PART I: LIFE IN A CAGE

Chapter 1: What Is a Cage?

"I Know Why the Caged Bird Sings"

~ *Maya Angelou*

The free bird leaps
on the back of the wind
and floats downstream
till the current ends
and dips his wings
in the orange sun rays
and dares to claim the sky.

But a bird that stalks
down his narrow cage
can seldom see through
his bars of rage
his wings are clipped and

his feet are tied
so he opens his throat to sing.

The caged bird sings
with fearful trill

of the things unknown
but longed for still
and his tune is heard
on the distant hill for the caged bird
sings of freedom.

The free bird thinks of another breeze
and the trade winds soft through the sighing trees
and the fat worms waiting on a dawn-bright lawn
and he names the sky his own.

But a caged bird stands on the grave of dreams
his shadow shouts on a nightmare scream
his wings are clipped and his feet are tied
so he opens his throat to sing.

The caged bird sings
with a fearful trill
of things unknown
but longed for still
and his tune is heard
on the distant hill
for the caged bird
sings of freedom.

In "Caged Bird," poet Maya Angelou describes first the joy of a bird free to soar through the sky and then describes a bird with clipped wings. Its feet have been tied, and, placed in a cage, it's unable to fly away. Yet, the caged bird continues to sing of freedom. She contrasts the struggles of the caged bird with the freedom of the free bird.

What Is a Cage?

A cage is a structure or enclosure in which someone or something is confined. A cage limits and restricts. For a bird, a cage keeps it from flying high and soaring. It keeps it boxed in. For a lion, it keeps it from roaming about and being the instinctive beast it naturally it. For bears, it keeps them limited and bored, and they often just give up and become inactive. A cage traps you, keeping you from the freedom to be true to yourself and becoming what life intended for you to be.

Physical, Emotional and Mental Cages

People have *physical, emotional and mental cages* that limit them in life.

Physical cages, such as jail and prison, keep us locked away from our families. They keep us confined. Ironically, physical cages aren't the worst things in the world, though.

Physical cages don't entirely limit our potential as humans. We can still flourish mentally in physical cages. Nelson Mandela proved this to the world. He was able to grow and gain psychological freedom in prison.

We also have **emotional cages** that we are regularly imprisoned in; for instance, not being able to properly deal with our feelings/emotions and appropriately articulate them. Not being capable of comprehending them. A lot of people are sad but mask the sadness with anger. Emotional cages are a huge deal in today's society.

Mental cages are the worst things in the world. Mental cages keep us down and hinder us from freedom, preventing us from elevating, evolving and developing into something greater.

They keep us from roaming, exploring and reaching our full potential. They keep us caged, lost and locked out.

You can't grow while being imprisoned in a cage mentally; you can't progress or get better. Growth is on the other side of the mental cage.

Societal Cages

Societal cages are the cages that society seats you in. The limits society places on you, the rules "they" say you have to follow in society. The system, "the man" agenda that creates systematic oppression and caging. As an African American athlete, I've been told that I'm not supposed to write a book— or be as articulate as I am.I broke out of those cages of the "typical-athlete." Most athletes are only focused on sports; they have no identity and most are string-puppets. I'm a well-rounded athlete. I used athletics as a vehicle to take me places.

Gender-Role Cages

We get put into gender cages as well. Men are taught to ONLY be combatants and savages. Women are taught to be sympathetic, subservient and subordinate. If a women steps out of this role and wants to be a boss or leader, she's viewed as the B-word. Men are taught to be tough and emotionless. If you step out of this role as a man, you're seen as weak or inferior. You can break out of these cages, though. It's okay for women to be bosses and stable, and its okay for men to be strong without being violent. That doesn't make you soft. Being in cages of savages, entitlement and emotionless teaching is the reason why men are the number one threat to women—not breast cancer, but men.

Blind to Being in a Cage

Unfortunately, you can be in a cage and not realize it, especially if you were born in a cage. That's most people's issue in the world. Take people who were born into poverty and oppression in the hood. They don't know they're caged because nobody has helped or shown them a better way; most of them have never been outside their environment.

A lot of schools educate poorly and aren't making room for critical thinking, so most kids are leaning on their own understanding. In their world, mediocrity is the norm—and very few work hard. On the flip side, take people who are born with riches and have had things handed to them in life—they also can be caged. They're caged to ignorance and entitlement. Not fulfilling their potential because they're spoiled. Not actually knowing they are in a cage and that they can break out of it.

Chapter 2: What's Your Cage?

Like most, you probably have different kinds of cages in your life, self-inflicted wounds that hurt and create self-doubt and blame.

Maybe you feel caged by addictions, fears or self-destructive habits. Maybe you feel caged by entitlement, thinking the world owes you everything and you don't have to work for anything.

Or you may be caged to following the norms of society and living up to what society says we are supposed to be and the expectations of others.

Or you may be caged in a relationship that you feel helpless to break out of or a dead end job that you can't seem to leave. Many people are caged in a negative self-image, thinking they don't deserve better. Some people are caged in mediocrity like I had been, not pushing to be our very best. The sad thing is many of us are happy with being mediocre, caged in and just going through the motions. We have to realize we were made to be so much more.

Some people talk on social media about wanting to break out of mediocrity and be great, but their habits don't match their work ethic.

The list goes on and on.

What is your cage? What limits you?

To find out mine, I had to look at my life and really think about what was keeping me caged. I know during my childhood, my cage was my attitude. Coming from Montbello, my friends and I didn't have a positive role model to look up to; we always had to be "Hard" and "Tough." It was a rough place, and I developed an attitude.

Having an attitude isn't all bad; however, when the attitude starts to affect your success and life, that's when it becomes a problem. My attitude kept me from so many opportunities. I would catch an attitude over the silliest things. I remember my aunt came in town and wanted to take my cousins and me to a NBA game.

I caught an attitude before going because I couldn't get the front seat in the car. So, I made a scene, opted not to go and ruined any future opportunities of going with my aunt. I caught attitudes in sports, school and everywhere else. As long as I had an attitude, I would remain mediocre and never become great.

I would be confined in my cage and held back from succeeding in school, sports and beyond. This attitude/ hothead cage kept me mediocre. I honestly didn't realize I was in a cage until my fateful meeting with Coach.

Luckily, I was able to break out of this cage because I had Coach as my big brother, mentor and guide at the age of 19— and to this very day.

He didn't give me money, he didn't give me handouts, and he didn't baby me. He helped me break out my cage of mediocrity, which led to me breaking out of tons of cages I was inside of, simply by inspiring me to change my paradigm.

Coach taught me to be my own person and not follow what everybody else is doing. A lot of guys were getting in trouble for trying to fit in. Coach taught me to stand out. All of this was far more valuable to me than money and any handout.

After this talk, my life changed, and since then, I've broken out of many cages, though I still have many more I need to break free from. For example, social media is a cage. I often get caught in the propaganda and the comparing of my life to others. I'll also find myself spending A LOT of time on it.

Coach opened my eyes to the difference between activity and productivity. You can't just be active, you have to be productive. I wasn't just being active; I started being productive and making the most of every opportunity. I became successful on the field. I gained a sixth sense in understanding the game and learned how to read defenses, get stronger, faster and break down film of other teams and myself. I didn't waste any plays and didn't leave anything on the field like I had in previous years.

Most importantly, after this talk, I become successful off the field as a person. I grew as a man, as a member of society, in my relationships—mentally, as my mind got sharper, emotionally, as I began to focus on positives. I grew both mentally and spiritually. I now make the most of every opportunity and maximize every opportunity I get in life, from mentoring to service, to my job and sports.

What is your cage (or cages)? To break out of your cage, you first need to recognize that you are in one. These questions will help you figure that out:

What's keeping me from mastering my craft?

What's keeping me from working a job I want, instead of settling?

What's keeping me from creating the best body I could have?

What's keeping me from starting my own business?

What's keeping me from financial success?

What's keeping me from finding true love?

What's keeping me from pursuing my dreams?

What's keeping me from contributing all I can for the greater good?

Write down your answers so you can figure out all the cages that keep you imprisoned.

_____

_____

PART II: BREAKING OUT OF YOUR CAGE

Chapter 3: Finding Out Your Why, Your Purpose

"He who has a why to live for can bear almost any how."
~ Friedrich Nietzsche

Do you have a life's purpose? Do you know your "why," the reason you do what you do? Most of us don't. Instead, we go through the motions like caged lions. In fact, most people spend more time planning their vacation than planning their life.

Don't be one of these people, or you will never get yourself out of your cage. Instead, you will drift along lost, constantly taking wrong turns down bumpy roads going nowhere, and you will wind up accomplishing little.

INSPIRING WORDS: "One day your life will flash before your eyes. Make sure it's worth watching." *~Unknown*

You must discover the purpose in life to give you the motivation to break free. Don't follow anybody else's rules and guidelines for you. Find your own purpose.

For me, my family is my why, as they depend on me for their welfare. I have a huge family that begins with my grandparents, Virgil and Mary Toombs. My grandparents work too hard for me not to be great. They are my why, along with the rest of my family. They motivate and push me. They are the reason I strive to be great. My grandparents adopted and fostered over 200 kids and changed many lives. Seeing them do this over time inspired me. I saw how caring and helping others can have an impact on people's lives. This is why I love to empower others for a living. This is how I discovered my purpose in life.

To break free and know your purpose in life, ask yourself what you'll live for—and even die for. Make a list of things you love. Soul search. Find what's important to you.

_____

_____

_____

_____

_____

_____

_____

_____

The answer might surprise you! My brother soul searched and, after playing basketball for 10 years, realized that he was just doing it because the family wanted him to. He wanted to go into business because he loved business, learning and sportswear.So he gave up basketball and started his own sportswear brand called "Celos" and went to school for marketing. It didn't matter what other people were telling him. He knew what was in his soul. He chose business over basketball and his passion, purpose and dreams over other people's plans, cages and viewpoints for him.

My sister's story is similar. She was a great soccer player growing up. Everybody just knew she would be a professional soccer player; she was fully capable of going pro. However, she soul searched and discovered that her passion was social work. This passion developed from seeing my grandparents and the amazing work that they did.

My sister is currently pursuing a master's degree in social work at Howard University. She's changing the world and impacting young people. Her way! Working hard, making moves and fulfilling her purpose in life.

This book has many strategies to help you find your purpose.
The very first one is to create a compelling vision for yourself.

"The two most important days in your life are the day you were born and the day you figure out why."

~Mark Twain

Tip 1: Explore Your Passion

What do you desire from your life? What gets you fired so there's no stopping you? To find out your personal vision, ask yourself the following questions:

Vision Questions:

1. **What is my ultimate dream?**
2. **If there was nothing holding me back, what would I want most?**
3. **Who are mt heroes?**
4. **What would I regret not having tried?**
5. **What would I do for free?**

Hopefully, you now feel closer to knowing your personal vision and what can help you break free from your cage. If not, you likely will by the end of this chapter, so don't worry. You'll get there.

Tip 2: Explore What Would Most Make You Feel Free from Your Cage

Everyone wants to feel free and in control of their lives, in other words, successful. We each have a different idea of what would make us feel free and successful.

What is yours? Make a list five things in order of priority that would make you feel free from your cage. Maybe it's a million dollars. Maybe it's getting a college degree. Maybe an athletic scholarship. Or maybe it's the status of being a CEO of a large company. Figure it out!

Make a list of five things:

_____

_____

_____

_____

_____

Tip 3: Take Advantage of Your Strengths

What are your strong points, what are you good at? Think about it. You might come up with things about yourself that you hadn't realized.

For instance, a close friend named "EC3" used to love to make musical beats, but he never realized he had a talent for it. Then one day he made up a beat for his brother and musical artist Tony C-Ali and his Cousin B.H2 dots. They loved it. Suddenly, everyone in the city was reaching out to hear my friend's production and beats. Eventually, he started publishing and producing music all over the nation. If he hadn't made up that beat for his brother, he might never have realized this talent.

What might you be good at that you have not realized? Most likely, it's something that comes naturally and easy to you. Perhaps it's astronomy, basketball, drawing, or business.

Make a list of all the things you do well. Write them out.

_____

_____

_____

_____

_____

_____

_____

_____

Don't be self-critical in the process. Don't think, "Yeah I do that okay but other people do it better." Just list your strengths. Remember, people are smart in different ways. You may be unable to utter an articulate sentence, but can sing like Beyoncé or Bruno Mars. Don't focus on what you can't do. Focus on what you're good at and put all your effort into developing those skills.

Tip 4: Create Your Life Purpose Statement

Write out an actual *Life Purpose Statement*. This = makes a difference. For President John Kennedy, it was to put a man on the moon by the end of 1960's. For Mohammed Ali, it was to be the greatest fighter. For Einstein, it was to solve the mystery of space and time. For myself, my life purpose statement is to break people out the cage.

What were you born to do?

Once you write your *Life Purpose Statement*, suddenly your whole life will have a clear direction. You will know what degree is best for you to pursue. You will know where on the planet is ideal for you to live. You will know the best career path to pursue.

Tip 5: Follow Your Inner Guidance System

"Happiness is not a goal; it is a by-product.
~Eleanor Roosevelt

If you want to break out of your cage, do what makes you happy, as happiness will propel you to take the actions needed to become a success.

Of course, only a tiny few of us *are* truly happy, right? Why? It's obvious. We're stuck in a cage and we let others dictate our dreams. Or we follow someone else's dream. For instance, my brother could have become a basketball player to please the family and not fulfill his dream of going into business. My sister could have played soccer to please her peers and not achieve her passion for social work.

Someone else might be stuck in another country because this is what your husband or wife wanted and you feel caged like a bird.

Break out of your cage. Don't follow someone else's version of what to do with your life. Follow your own inner guidance system.

If you're unsure, listen to your intuition. If you feel bored, drained, or just want to get out of where you're at, follow your gut and get out! If something doesn't feel right for you and you continue the activity, you will never break free but remain feeling negative about yourself, unhappy and even depressed. Don't let this happen to you. Be sure that what you want matches your values and your life purpose.

Don't live someone else's dream!

Most importantly, enjoy the moments! I remember always wanting to go on to the next thing, the next stage and phase. I didn't appreciate where I was at in life. In middle school, I was ready for high school; in high school, I was ready for college and in college, ready for the pros/graduation. I never really appreciated the moment. We have to appreciate the moment.

Tip 6: Find Your "Coach" Muse

All of us have creative energy within us. If you wish to break out of your cage, tap into and explore your source of creativity. Let your muses fly and life will become exciting. A muse is someone who inspires you to achieve things, to do better and to have success. Find your muse.

In the morning, you won't roll out of bed but jump out. Boredom is now history, as are depression and despair.

My bro Blake Swain always wanted start his own brand and expand his possibilities. He wanted to begin his own enterprise (comedy, photography, videography, entertainment and podcasting, etc.)

In high school he was a star in both football and basketball. He even received a D1 full-ride athletic scholarship to Colorado State University. Though he excelled in football, he didn't know if he should go for his dream of beginning his brand in business/entertainment because football was his identity.

Then his friend O'Brian, who was also a star athlete who shared the same passions for comedy, photography, videography, and podcasting, encouraged him to go for it, and the two became each other's muses. They encouraged and pushed each other. Today, Blake has his own business, "Swain Visions." He is also one of the most polished and successful comedians from the city.

In addition, he is branching out and taking over the photography scene. OB and Blake both broke out of their cages of being labeled "athletes."

It is true that some people are more innovative than others. But talent for something lies within us all, even if you don't become LeBron James, Drake or Steve Jobs. Find yours!

Tip 7: Get Inspired

"Everyone can rise above their circumstances if they're passionate about what they do."

~ Nelson Mandela

What inspires you? Perhaps it's going to a NFL game or listening to a lecture by Eric Thomas on how to succeed. (I personally listen to lectures by Dr. Bounce Back "G.O.T.H" or Jonathon McMillian "BTA" and get inspired). Whatever it is, take advantage of it to get inspired. This will expand your horizons so anything seems possible and at your reach.

SUMMING UP

Before you can feel motivated to break out of your cage, you need to find your purpose in life, the reason why you are on this earth.

Here are steps to help you do this:

- Create a compelling vision by exploring your passion and figuring out what would most make you feel free from your cage.

- Take advantage of your strengths in figuring out your life purpose.

- Create your life purpose statement.

- Follow your inner guidance system by going with what your heart tells you.

- Find your "coach" muse, someone to inspire your journey.

- Get inspired by listening to and reading about people you greatly admire.

As you think about these things, write them down.

_____

_____

_____

_____

_____

_____

_____

_____

Chapter 4: Run Your Own Race

GO AT YOUR OWN PACE

Turtle Mode

I remember sitting in on the *Life Is Dope* podcast. This is an amazing international podcast. Weekly, hosts Graffiti & Davey bring you honest and opinionated perspectives on current events, music, news and everything DOPE with unique figures. This week it was with Trev Rich, a hot new hip-hop artist.

Trev is one of the dopiest artists to come out of the West coast, a musician signed to one of the most amazing labels in history, *Cash Money Records*. He said it took him 15 years to get a deal. Yes. For 15 years, he was rapping and grinding before he got signed.

He had to work hard each day and sometimes choose between his next meal and studio time. It was a struggle especially because people would tell him to stop dreaming and go out and get a job. He almost gave up 1,000 times, but he kept going.

Listening to the podcast and sitting up close and personal, his journey became inspiring. It was obvious how hard he worked and pushed no matter how slow things were moving. It was a vicarious experience for me, just listening to him talk about it. An important tip: things don't just happen. There's no overnight success. It takes time and dedication. You have to embrace your turtle mode.

My Turtle Mode

I remember the day I was sent to private school as a result of fighting too much. The teachers and councilors were worried about me. They thought it better for me to go to a private school.

I was so disappointed. I didn't know why this was happening to me. The school I went to required that I take a test to get placed. My test scores were low. This meant that I started out behind and had to take "special classes" to catch up to the other kids.

Everybody was so far ahead of me. What a grind! I had to work twice as hard as the other kids over the years. Kids were passing me up, but I kept going. Though I excelled on the football field, I didn't receive any football offers, and everybody got signed to a major Division One School except me. D1 is the highest level of college football and the most prestigious and recognized. I was the MVP (Most Valuable Player) of the team that year, yet I was still overlooked.

I kept going at my pace, though. I kept moving.

Eventually, I caught up to everybody.

But they soon left me again, as everybody but me had scholarships. I chose to go to Kansas State to study engineering because they were the only one out of 37 schools that accepted me—every other college denied me. I didn't receive a football scholarship, either. I still kept moving.

I dropped out my freshmen year at Kansas State. Don't get me wrong—it was a great campus and a great school. It's just that I didn't have enough money and I broke my wrist the fifth day of football practice. I was a walk-on so I didn't get the treatment like everyone else.

"Walk-on" means I'm on the team, but without a scholarship. That meant I had to pay for everything myself, unlike the other athletes on scholarship who got food, housing, and medical all paid for.

I was upset. My mom, however, didn't let me come home to Colorado, so I had to stay in Kansas.

Luckily, My Uncle Virgil lived there and let me stay with him on his farm. I lived in my uncle's basement and sat and watched as my teammates, kids I grew up with and others I'd met, were all living out their dreams—all at colleges, playing ball, studying in school. They were balling and I was in my uncle's basement.

I almost stopped running my race. I almost quit. But the story of the tortoise and the hare always stayed with me—how the slow and steady tortoise ended up winning the race.

I kept going. I was moving slow, but I was moving. I was in turtle mode.

Taking Action

The key to getting ahead is getting started. It's action! I applied to Barton Community College (Fort Riley, KS) and in my first semester, I failed two of my classes, classes that I was capable of passing.

However, I didn't really apply myself, and I felt I shouldn't be there at that school. But it was a wake-up call. The following semesters, I got all A's. I started going to office hours. Office hours are one-on-one time with your teacher or professor.

It's a time where you can receive more teaching, more help and the benefit of the doubt. And I started to really apply myself.

Turtle mode wasn't just about moving slow. It was about moving, but making sure I got better with each move. My GPA went from a 1.8 to a 3.5. I applied to the University of Colorado and I got accepted! I also applied for academic scholarships and got them, as well. There is so much free money out there in the world—take advantage!

At the University of Colorado, I felt I had a great opportunity at redemption, especially when I looked around and saw that the people I grew up with, the people from high school, were slowly falling off. They were failing in school, getting kicked off teams and not able to get back on track.

I was catching up slowly, as I was running my own race at my own pace. I got to join the University of Colorado football team. It was a dream come true! However, I was the eighth running back on the depth chart, and it didn't look like I was going to last.

I just kept working and moving at my pace.

When I failed, I took that as a learning opportunity to figure out my mistakes and improve. I began to excel in all my classes, not because I was smarter or better, but because I knew the importance of the opportunity and I applied myself.

I asked questions. I worked hard in the weight room and was always in the film room, looking over plays, and understanding that in the off-season, that's how you win. This is how I moved up the depth chart.

I went from 8th to 2nd on the depth chart as a sophomore. I earned a football scholarship—and I kept going.

Eventually, I passed up the people that were ahead of me. I ran my own race. I didn't rush and I understood that things take time. I never gave up.

You have to be in turtle mode. It's not about moving slowly, it is about moving at your own pace.

We often get off track when we try to run at other peoples' pace and we pay attention to their race. We forget about our race or we start to compare our race to others, and that doesn't help at all. To break out the cage, realize it's okay to move slowly. Just don't give up. Embrace turtle mode.

Run your own race! Run at your own pace! Persist until you break out of that cage and fly free.

SUMMING UP

The best way to succeed is by embracing your turtle mode. Like me, you need to keep going, but at your own pace. If you do this, you will eventually catch up to everybody and even fly ahead of them.

Remember, turtle mode isn't just about moving slowly. It's about moving and making sure that you get better with each move. Ask questions. Work hard and keep going.

Most importantly, run your own race, not someone else's. Don't rush. Understand that things take time. Don't ever give up.

Run your own race! Run at your own pace!

Chapter 5: Become Your Authentic Self

When I take my little homies, my mentees and my younger family members to visit college campuses, corporations and businesses, they think those things aren't for them, that they don't have what it takes to succeed, that they aren't good enough.

I try to get them to understand that they *are* good enough, that they can get what they want. Succeeding won't be easy. The world isn't a fairytale. But if you put in the work, follow your heart and are resilient, you can break out of your cage and have what you want in life. You can't wish for it, you can't just dream and pray. You have to go get it.

And the way to get it is by becoming your authentic self. This is what got Oprah Winfrey started.

When Oprah Winfrey started working as the late-night anchor on WLAC-TV in Nashville, Tenn., she was so young that she still had an 11 p.m. curfew at home. Only a 19-year-old, she recited the news on camera so successfully that in no time, a television station in Atlanta offered her $40,000 to come to them, quadrupling her salary.

She turned it down. Her manager in Nashville told her she needed to stay there until she could write better and perfect her craft as a journalist.

She agreed and didn't take the job. Not because she couldn't take on a new challenge but because, as she later said, "I could feel inside myself ... that he was absolutely right." At that moment, she had "started listening to what felt like the truth to me."

And the truth, she later figured out was that she was better at chatting up ice cream vendors than covering murders, and realizing that, after 25 years of non-stop being *Oprah*, she also realized that it was time to end her wildly popular daytime talk show and start OWN – Oprah Winfrey Network.

Don't Compare Yourself to Others

Don't chase other people's dreams because you think they are better than yours. Do what you're good at.

Learn to Say No

Maintain self-boundaries. If something isn't good for you, say no. Don't try to please others.

Believe in Yourself

A lot of people today look at social media and see all these presumably perfect people who have it all: good looks, money, fame, beautiful spouses, everyone looking as if it came easily, without a struggle. After seeing this social media utopia, people then feel discouraged and give up trying because they think they can never compete and there's no point in even trying.

Social media isn't real; don't let it dictate your life.

I spend a lot of my time mentoring at a youth center. When I started off, I started bringing people to speak to the youth from prestigious places. I would think the kids loved the speeches and seemed to be responding well. However, the kids would only feel more discouraged because they felt that they couldn't be perfect like the speakers. The speakers I invited never shared any adverse times or any challenges. The kids couldn't relate because they saw no struggle.

Their response was, "I'd rather not try at all than try and fail."

I once was caged with this exact mindset; more accurately, I was self-caged. When I got told "no" or rejected, I shut down. I lacked resilience to bounce back. I lacked the mental fortitude to keep going or push through.

I broke out of this cage by watching my Aunt Nina hang her college rejection letters up, so everybody could see. She also posted them on social media, her clipboard and calendar.

At the time I didn't understand why. Confused, I asked her, "Auntie, these are negative. Why are you posting them?"

Her answer impacted me hugely. She told me she uses them as motivation to show that, even though she was an accomplished teacher, graduate and leader, she still gets rejected—but doesn't let it stop her.

That revelation helped make me more resilient. She showed me the power of perseverance, and this helped me break out of my self-caging stage.

I started applying these traits daily and it helped out. I got rejected so many times, but I still kept trying, and eventually, I broke through. When I fell down, I got back up. The best thing I ever did was believe in myself.

You have to believe in you! You are unique. You were created to be great. You have a purpose for being on this earth.

Each summer, my uncle took seven of us (my brothers/cousins) to his farm in Kansas to keep us out of the streets and trouble. He took care of us and helped us break out of all our different cages. I didn't realize it at the time, but Uncle Virgil was the reason I was able to excel in football. He didn't let me sell myself short at all. He knew about the cage, just like Coach did. But you know, we don't listen to our family at times because we are hardheaded (at least I am).

Uncle V taught us the power of belief. He believed in us more then we believed in ourselves, and that helped us to learn to believe in ourselves. He also believed in himself even when others didn't and that inspired us. If he said he was going to do something, he did it. For example, if he said he was going to build a fence, he would build a fence. He did everything he said he would set out to do.

Coming from the inner city of Montbello, Uncle V was still able to accomplish much. Growing up, he was one of the best athletes to come out the state. Now he owns a farm and is a man of great faith. To me, he is a living model of the credo: if you believe in yourself, nobody can stop you!

I remember we had to run 10 miles every day at Uncle V's house. I would always come in 3rd place of the 7 running. My uncle would always ask me, "Nephew, why didn't you come in first?"

I thought he was crazy, but he really believed in me and saw my potential. He told me to believe in myself! He showed me that the body follows the mind. After talking to him and telling myself I could come in first, I put it in my head that I would come in first. I believed I could.

Now, when you plant a seed, the fruit doesn't show up right away. However, I was watering this seed of winning and doing my best in the race. About a week and a half following the talk with my uncle, I started coming in first place.

My uncle told me, "All it took was believing. When you truly believe in yourself, the body follows and habits change." I didn't just say "I believe." I told myself I could, and my actions followed. I wasn't sitting around drinking soda and eating candy. I drank more water and stretched, I prepared myself to win way before the challenge even began.

And I focused on what I wanted to do. And where focus goes, energy flows. I started believing even before we ran—and that's where I won.

You have to believe in yourself to break out the cage. None of my family thought I could come in first, but time after time, I did. Mark and Chris (my two older cousins) would always win. But once I told myself I could... I did.

Even if everybody around you is failing and not doing right, you still have to believe in yourself. If you do, you can break out of the cage. And I'm going to help you through this journey.

WRITE YOUR STORY

Step 1: Start fresh. Write out your story as it is right now in all areas: body image, relationships, health, work, career, community, finances.

Step 2: Now, write out your story as you would like it to be.

Step 3: Think of your life as a work in progress. After you finish reading this book, write out your *new* story. Be prepared to be astonished at all the changes!

Accept Failure. We all take losses in life. Success rarely comes without first losing. If you are unhappy in your job, explore new possibilities. If someone's holding you back from reaching your potential, pack up and dip.

Thrive on the Challenge. As Rodney Billups, head men's basketball coach at the University of Denver, always says, "Tough times don't last, tough people do." Understand that challenges come daily. It is how you respond to the challenges that set the winners apart from the losers. Take on new challenges. Never be surprised, and know that you or your team can only become stronger by overcoming a challenge.

Break out the Cage. Break from what's holding you back in life. Challenges will make you or break you. Don't run from problems. Become free of what's holding you back. Always remember where you come from doesn't dictate where you're headed in life.

Tip 4: Embrace Failure

"The greatest glory in living lies not in never falling, but in rising every time we fall."

~ Nelson Mandela

Failure is actually your best friend, if you use it to learn. It gives you an opportunity to learn from your mistakes. It forces you to take a different road that you might not have taken. Rather than complaining about how things didn't work out, think of failure as an opportunity.

This will help you become willing to risk failures. Einstein said, "Success is failure in progress." Thinking back to when I dropped out of Kansas State University, I was at rock bottom and felt like a total failure. My bro Kristian told me not to let "failure go to my heart or success go to my head." He told me that failure isn't permanent unless I allow it to be.

I felt like a failure, but he showed me that it was a chance to analyze the process and decisions I had made; it was a chance to learn and grow. He showed me that I could pick a new school or go back. He helped me map out my future and make a plan.

INSPIRING WORDS: *"It's fine to celebrate success but it is more important to heed the tips of failure." ~Bill Gates*

When you fail, figure out what went wrong. If you can't, ask experts and browse the Internet for solutions. Keep trying to figure out how you could have done things differently. The next time the situation comes up, you will know what to do better. And if not, each time you fail, you will discover one new thing that prevented you from succeeding. After enough failures, nothing will stand in your way.

INSPIRING WORDS: *"Success is how high you bounce when you hit bottom." ~General George Patton*

SUMMING UP

The most important thing in life is to live it as your authentic self. Don't live someone else's dreams. Don't compare yourself to others. Believe in yourself and become your best friend.

Think of your life as a work in progress. Rewrite your story and become the person you were meant to be.

And remember, to become your true self, you have to be willing to take risks and accept failure.

Chapter 6: Have a Positive Mindset

"What we think we become." ~Buddha

I've been talking about the need to believe in yourself, to ignore self-criticism and plow ahead to meet your destiny. To do so, you need to be careful about the words you feed yourself.

Inside your head is an on-going inner dialogue. It makes up your story and is based on how you perceive your world and yourself. These words are incredibly powerful. They create your reality and need to be chosen carefully because they become your self-image, defining who you are and unconsciously guiding daily actions and decisions. They create the story of your life.

How do you want your story to read? Like a bird free of its cage, flying happily wherever it wishes to go? Or a captive one whose story will be forever hidden and unknown?

If you want it to read like a free bird, you will have to ensure that your inner dialogue is mostly positive: "I'm smart." "I'm able to get what I want." "I'm interesting." "I'm capable of doing what I need to do to get ahead."

If not, and your mind-chatter tends to be mostly negative – "They're better than me," "I'm fat," "I can't," "I'm ugly," "I'm stupid." "I never finish anything," "I will never succeed." – you will remain a caged bird and feel you have no control over your destiny.

The choice is yours.

Basically, it comes down to the "Law of Attraction," which is: *Positivity attracts more positivity; negativity attracts more negativity.* This law affects every area of your life—your health, wealth, happiness and relationships.

How to Program Your Mind to Break Free from Your Cage

Your mind is like a computer. What you put in is what comes out. If your inner chatter that runs through your head keeps telling you that you will never become successful, fit, rich, happy, fulfilled, or anything special, you will remain trapped inside your cage—obsessing over paying your bills, worried you're going to mess up, pondering over whether you will get fired from your job, or if you'll get cut.

And this, as you can guess, strengthens the worry function in your brain and keeps you locked up into "I can't," "I suck." And so you just keep obsessing, dragging, losing sleep, feeling sorry for yourself and making others around you miserable. Without realizing it, you are pushing away the people and resources you need to get what you want and sabotaging your chances of breaking free.

If the chatter says, "I can be rich, successful, happy, and intelligent," you will attract the people and resources you need to meet your goals and fly enthusiastically to success.

WISE WORDS: *"It is better to light a candle than curse the darkness." ~Eleanor Roosevelt*

Neuroplasticity

And this really can happen because of something called "neuroplasticity," which is the brain's ability to be endlessly adaptable and dynamic.

When you are a free bird, you think, act and have a positive attitude. You tell yourself, "I'm winning!" "I can get what I want!" "I am the master of my fate!"

And when this is your inner dialogue, your brain releases feel-good hormones that increase the number of branches and synaptic connections in the hippocampus, the area of the brain responsible for memory. Over time, these areas strengthen and change your brain so that positive thinking and going for what you want becomes a natural part of you.

Embrace life with hope, optimism and good energy. Live a longer, more satisfying and successful life!

WISE WORDS: *"Let our advance worrying become advance thinking and planning." ~Winston Churchill*

Effect of Emotions on the Body

To give you a taste of what happens when you are locked in a cage, look in the mirror and think of a worst-case scenario. Think of all the haters. Think of your dream being taken away. Did you see how your facial expression changed? How you began to frown, how your eyebrows furrowed, your shoulders tensed up and your hands clenched? Notice also how your breathing became quick and shallow. This is what being caged does to you.

Now think of something that makes you happy. Notice how your expression changes, your body relaxes, your breathing deepens and slows and your fists unclench. This is what happens to your body when you break out of your cage.

You Have the Power

You have the power to break free from your cage. All you have to do is to change your thinking to a positive mindset. Once you do, the door will open and you can fly away.

You have the power! You can do it!

Here's How

When it comes to thinking positively, less is not more. In fact, the more you entertain a positive thought and positive energy, the more powerful it becomes.

For instance, let's say you are working hard at building up your running speed, but you keep running into roadblocks that keep you from flying down the field. If every time this happens, you announce to yourself, "I can do it. I just need to persist," this positive thought will become your belief. Look what happened to me!

But if, instead, you put time, attention and energy into negative thoughts, and keep telling yourself that you are too short, too slow or that your legs aren't long enough for the necessary stride, the negative or unwanted thoughts will override the positive.

True, things are not likely to change overnight. You might at times continue to self-cage. But luckily, we all have the capacity to create new programs and revise old programs in our brains. You do this by repeatedly refusing to believe the negative thinking that goes on inside your head, over and over.

Over time, these negative, self-caging thoughts will slowly diminish and be replaced by more rational, balanced thinking.

Have an Attitude of Gratitude

Feel thankful for the things you have rather than bitter about the things you don't have. We'll talk more about gratitude a bit later.

Choose Your Battles

Don't add to the stress in your life by having a meltdown if the waiter takes too long to bring your dinner or if traffic is moving slow. Go with the flow or, as the saying goes, don't sweat the small stuff. Learn to react and when to use your energy.

Obstacles are Opportunities

Obstacles are your best friends because they are an opportunity for personal growth and breaking out of the cage. As Nietzsche said...

"That which does not kill us makes us stronger."

When you've made a poor choice that turned out badly, don't hit yourself over the head. Reflect on your choice and learn from your mistakes. Every time you think a negative thought, ask yourself, "How is this serving me?" For real. If it doesn't, let it go.

Surround Your Life with Good Energy

If things make you snap, jumpy or negative, don't engage in them. If listening to the news annoys or angers you, turn off the TV. If traffic unnerves you, take a different, less-traveled route. If walking through a mall stresses you, shop online. If the flexing on social media makes you mad, log off.

Fill your life with music you love, films that inspire you, sports that get you charged up and excited.

Avoid gossip whenever possible. Our brains cannot distinguish between that which is real and that which is imagined. If we listen to doses of complaints from co-workers about other co-workers, the effect on the brain is the same as if we had lived those experiences ourselves.

Hang Out with the Like-minded

Be very selective about who you spend time with. Look for upbeat, optimistic people who spread good energy, rather than the naysayers and haters. Share your optimism with them and gently direct conversations in a constructive direction when it starts to turn ugly.

Banish False Beliefs

"If it's never our fault, we can't take responsibility for it. If we can't take responsibility for it, we'll always be its victim."
~Richard Bach

Do you slip into thinking of yourself as a victim, with little or no control over your life? Many people do. You feel sorry for yourself, as the world seems to be against you. Stuck in self-pity, you take little to no action and you get lost in sadness and self-pity.

To break free of the "I'm a victim" cage – the victim mindset — it is absolutely necessary that you break free from the "poor me, I'm a victim" mode.

How can you do that? There are many ways.

Recognize the Benefits of a Victim Mentality
Get attention Being a victim produces concern and caring from other people who try to help you out. On the other hand, it may not last for that long, as people get tired of it.

Can play it safe People who feel like victims tend to not take action. Without trying and taking action, you don't have to risk rejection or failure. You don't have to worry about any discomfort of stepping out and trying new responses.

<u>Don't have to take responsibility</u> It's easier to blame others than to take personal responsibility for your actions.

Free Yourself From The Benefits Listed Above

Let go of the benefits that come from being a victim/survivor. It might be hard at first to not forever be talking about everything that's wrong in your life, how life has treated you cruelly, how you have rotten luck. How so many people have wronged you.

But you must take this first step and take responsibility for your actions.

Vow to fill your life with new thinking that may feel uncomfortable at first but is necessary for growth.

Be Aware

First and foremost, be aware that you are playing the "woe is me" victim. Only then, will you be able to take steps to break free and take flight down a different, more satisfying path and move forward.

Take Responsibility for Your Life

"In the long run, we shape our lives, and we shape ourselves. The process never ends until we die. And the choices we make are ultimately our own responsibility."
~Eleanor Roosevelt

No matter how much you may want to blame others for your problems, it gets you nowhere. You will never break out of your cage until you take responsibility for the choices you make, good or bad.

Assigning blame and making excuses will only keep you victimized. You don't have to do anything different because it's not about you. It's about someone or something else. You're only the recipient.

If you don't break out of this mindset and take responsibility for your life and own it, you will continue to feel like a caged bird and blame everyone else for your bondage. And you will never take actions to change if you don't own up to them.

You will remain stuck and continue to complain and feel miserable in your status quo of negativity. You must own up to your life as your responsibility. Only you can take the steps needed to break out of your cage and fly free.

Once you do, you will also find that you will stop relying on external validation like praise from other people to feel good about yourself. Instead, you build inner stability and a ton of positive emotions, no matter what other people say or do around you.

Steps to take to begin taking responsibility for your life:

One: Decide to take on a different mindset.

Two: Decide that your life is up to you.

Three: Read some great books, or listen to great audio tapes by people like Eric Thomas, Dudley Thurmond, Raven Turner, and, of course, Gary V.

Four: Apologize for something sincerely without attaching "and" or "but" to it. For instance, "I'm sorry I yelled, but I couldn't help myself." The "but" disqualifies the apology. Take responsibility for having yelled.

Five: Empower yourself with "I will" and "I can" statements. "I can give this presentation." "I will start this podcast." This will get things flowing and fill you with positive energy.

If, instead, you put up stop signs of "I won't" and "I can't," you cut off any creative thinking that might yield an unexpected, "Yes! I can do this."

Six: Adopt the attitude that change begins with you.

Have Gratitude

"If you don't think every day is a good day,
just try missing one."
~Robert Cavett

If you're like most, you tend to focus more on what you don't have than on what you do have. For instance, you might be mad at not having the newest car rather than be grateful for having a car with good mileage that rarely needs maintenance. If you feel grateful for what you do have, rather than dwelling on what you don't have, your life will take on different meaning and perspective. If not, you will continue to feel like a victim and dwell on how everyone has it better than you. I'm not saying settle and be complacent. I'm saying be grateful and keep grinding.

Feel grateful for all the blessings you have in your life. Also, ask yourself when you're in a tough spot and you feel that the world has it out for you, what is the hidden opportunity to be learned here?

How can you become more grateful for what you have?

Do what NBA legend Chauncey Billups does — have an attitude of gratitude. Appreciate everything. Randomly and casually write down five things for which you feel grateful. Some days, your list will be filled with amazing things; other days, just simple enjoyments.

Here are some ideas:

-I am thankful for my eyes, my hands, my feet.

-I am grateful for Grandma's unconditional love.

-I am gratcful for my friends.

-I am grateful to have Uncle Virgil mentoring me.

-I am grateful for my good health.

-I am grateful for Grandpa's wisdom.

Forgive

"When you hold resentment toward another, you are bound to that person or condition by an emotional link that is stronger than steel. Forgiveness is the only way to dissolve that link and get free."
~Catherine Ponder

To stop feeling like a victim, you must try to forgive wrongdoings against you. If you don't, you will forever be linked to that person.

Constantly, you will think about how that person wronged you over and over again and feel angry. And you will suffer more than if you forgive them.

Focus on the needs of others

Help someone else out and give him or her value. This will get you out of the "poor me" mode.

SUMMING UP

You can program your mind to break free from your cage by learning to think positively and having gratitude. And your brain will change because of neuroplasticity—which, again, is the brain's ability to rewire itself.

You Have the Power. Use it! Here are the many ways:

-Reframe thoughts from negative to positive.

-Have an attitude of gratitude.

-Choose your battles so you don't sweat the small stuff.

-View setbacks as challenges.

-Surround your life with good energy and stay away from negative people.

-Hang out with the like-minded people.

-Most importantly, banish false beliefs and stop feeling you're a victim. Instead, take responsibility for your actions and behavior.

-Forgive those who have wronged you and focus on the needs of others, not just on yourself.

Chapter 7: Get Out of Your Comfort Zone

I was sitting and talking to my youngin' who was very upset. He was the star quarterback at his university. Though a lot of people doubted he would make it, he worked hard the previous year to earn that spot. And he started quarterback as a freshman as well, which was rare.

He did okay, but now, he told me his coaches had brought in transfer quarterbacks from other schools that are older and have more starts under their belts, more experience.

I stopped him immediately and asked, "So what's the problem?"

He said, "They want them to take my spot."

I told him, "They're applying that heat! The heat is good for you." I broke it down to him. It's like uncooked pizza dough or a pink steak.

Nobody wants something that hasn't been cooked. Nobody wants anything that hasn't had heat applied to it. Just like a pizza in the oven, you have to be cooked; you have to go through the heat so you can come out well done. The heat is good for you.

I told him, "Always keep an open mind. Without adversity, without pain, without heat, we wouldn't be able to grow and we'd stay the same. The heat, the pain, is where you'll see the most response, where you'll see the most action and where— most importantly—you'll break out of the cage."

For the heat challenges you to get better and become solid. Nobody thrives from a smooth path with no challenges. It's the challenge that really pushes us. Without pain we wouldn't be able to grow. If you stay safe in your comfort zone, you stay in your cage. You could be in a cage filled with love, and you're still in a cage.

Break Out of Your Comfort Zone

To get out of your comfort zone, experience something you're not used to. Try new things, learn something new, talk to somebody you normally wouldn't talk to, challenge yourself. You'll be more productive later on, you'll grow and the cage will be gone.

Every day, explore your limits by taking one small step outside your comfort zone.

Here are some ideas that have helped me and still help me to do just that.

Eat something unusual. Try a vegetarian dish at lunch in place of a burger.

Smile more. In place of going along with your day in your normal social way, make an effort to smile more—at your co-workers, the lady at the supermarket checkout, your kids.

Also, look in the mirror and smile to yourself. See what happens.

Try a different sound. If you only listen to hip-hop, try listening to R & B and vice versa. When you feel really daring, try listening to an opera.

Read something you never would have imagined reading. Try reading a biography of someone whose story doesn't directly apply to your life or interest, like Nelson Mandela.

Try a new sport. Try a sport that you don't have the skills for. If you are poor at speed and quick foot movement, try learning tennis. If you have an inflexible body, try taking yoga.

Take a class in public speaking. Public speaking is something almost everyone dreads. Challenge this fear by learning how to speak before an audience.

Watch something different. If you usually watch thrillers, then try a serious drama or romantic comedy.

Take a day offline. For many, few things will get us out of our comfort zone more than being offline for any extended period of time. Try it. It's a wonderful change of pace.

Take a vacation to a new place. Try to visit a place with a culture and lifestyle very different from yours.

Walk or bike to work. Instead of taking the car or riding the bus or train as usual, get some exercise and fresh air by walking or biking to work.

Walk away. Rather than getting into an argument or spiff and then replaying it over and over in your mind—what was said, could have been said differently—let it all go. Walk away.

Distract yourself from ruminating over and over about what happened. When an old memory pops up today, let it go instead of dwelling on it.

Get out of the house. If you usually stay in on Wednesday night, call up a few friends and head down to the local sports bar. Call up someone you haven't seen in ages and meet them for a cup of coffee.

Throw out anything you haven't worn or used in a year. Go through one part of your home at a time, like a closet or drawer in your desk. If you haven't used it in a year, toss it or give it to a friend or a charity.

SUMMING UP

The comfort zone is being in a cage. You could be in a cage filled with love, and you're still in a cage. Experience something you're not used to so you can get out of your cage.

Chapter 8: Break Out of Your Fear Cage

"I've had a lot of worries in my life,
most of which never happened."
~ Mark Twain

I had a fear of flying and that kept me caged for a while. I remember sitting with my Grandpa Virgil Toombs, Sr. He was so upset with me because it was summertime and I had missed yet another family reunion, and he wanted me to meet my other family members.

Family reunions were annual things. We lived in Colorado and all the family reunions were always in Washington, D.C., Maryland, Kansas or Virginia, and even one time in Connecticut.

But unless we drove, I would always miss them because of my fear of flying. If we weren't driving, I wasn't going!

My fear of flying kept me paralyzed and stuck in the same place and caused me to miss out on many opportunities. Yet, I didn't even realize this until my grandfather showed me his disappointment about my not flying, along with other family members who tried to encourage me to fly. They would tell me, "Everything will be okay."

My grandpa really opened my mind; I didn't realize I was caged by being scared to fly. I thought I was protecting myself. I was comfortable. I didn't like flying and I'd rather stay where I was. My grandfather even said, "Stop being caged and fly." What a wise man.

But I was too afraid and, consequently, I missed out on so many opportunities: camps, symposiums, workshops, retreats and vacations.

Plane rides are four to five hours, tops, and I didn't want to do it. My fear of flying came from fear of heights, a fear I had developed at a young age and it stuck with me. You could say it was "all in my head."

Fears Leave Us Caged

Do fears stop you from taking the steps needed to get what you want out of life? Like me, many people feel crippled by fear. We feel afraid of taking an elevator, starting a business like my brother did instead of sticking with sports. Or speaking up at work, thinking that we will be judged or even get fired, or doing an internship, thinking we will fail. And so we end up doing nothing, and we fail to grow.

True, some fears are inborn and necessary for survival, like fear of snakes, fire or strangers. But many of us are caged by fears inside our head that are often based on limiting personal beliefs that create dangerous negativity: "I can't do it," "I'm a failure," "I don't have the right stuff to succeed" or "They'll laugh at me."

Don't let your fears stop you from your dreams. Face and banish them now. If not, they will become a boa constrictor wrapped around you, squeezing and restricting you and leaving you stuck in self-doubt and limited beliefs. If fears fill your head, you can never advance and break out of your cage.

True, it's not easy getting past your fears, I know that all too well with my fear of flying. You will resist, we all do. But once you take the tiger by the tail, you can get past them. You will come to accept failure as inevitable, success as scary and rejection as a fact of life—but that's okay—you know you can work past it. Eventually, you will free yourself of your cage of self-defeating fears. You will accomplish what you want. I'm no longer afraid to fly. It was a long journey. Break out!

Basic Fears That Keep Us Caged

FEAR OF FAILURE

"You'll always miss 100% of the shots you don't take."
~Wayne Gretzky

Fear of failure is a very common fear. We avoid doing things and stay safe because we are convinced we will fail.

This fear is very crippling because it rules our actions and decisions. If we are too afraid to pursue our dreams because we are convinced we will fail, we don't take the necessary steps to become a warrior/leader. We may not even try.

Why We Fear Failure

Fear of failure comes from a fear of taking risks because you feel vulnerable. What if all your efforts to get a scholarship fail, or to get that cool date? Is it even worth trying again?

Failure Varies

Of course, what is failure for you might not feel like a failure to someone else. To some, an A- means failure, while for others it's getting a C. For some, getting only the silver medal at the Olympics means failure, while for others, it's not making one basket the whole game.

So, it really comes down to perspective.

BANISH YOUR FEAR OF FAILURE

Take Risks

"Go out on a limb. That's where the fruit is."
~ Jimmy Carter

Taking risks is absolutely essential to breaking out of your cage. How do you convince yourself to do this? You change your mindset to see failure as a stepping-stone, not an end in itself. When you fail, ask yourself what could you have done differently or better to achieve a different outcome. Said Thomas Edison, "I have not failed. I've just found 10,000 ways that won't work."

Always remember, when the going gets tough, the tough get going. Take risks and get going.

Accept Losing

Losing is part of becoming a success. Accept that it happens. If you feel you've failed at your job, look for a job that suits your talents and skills better. If your spouse holds you back from reaching your potential, hit the road, Jack.

Thrive on the challenge. Michael Jordan, arguably the greatest basketball player of all time, was cut from his high school basketball team. In multiple commercials, he says "I have missed more than 9,000 shots in my career. I have lost almost 300 games. On 26 occasions I have been entrusted to take the game-winning shot, and I missed. I have failed over and over and over again in my life. And that is why I succeed." Failure is temporary, unless you let it defeat you permanently.

Take the Bull by the Horns

You've heard of how someone learned how to swim by getting thrown into the middle of the lake and told: "Sink or swim!" Looking fear in the face and talking back to it is a powerful way to overcome any fear. Said Eleanor Roosevelt, "Do something that scares you every day."

This is how I overcame my fear of dogs. Growing up, Aunt Dee put me in the room with her and her dogs, J.C. and Max. They were two large, active German Shepherds. I was terrified the whole time. I was panicking and bugging out. But eventually, I calmed down and learned to not be afraid of them. After a couple of minutes, my fear of dogs was gone. Aunt Dee had reassured me—and proved to me—that it was all in my head.

Befriend the Worst-Case Scenario

Instead of fearing the worst-case scenario, consider all your options for taking the next step. Ask yourself, what's the worst that could happen if it doesn't go well? What's the worst possible outcome? What are some ways to handle it differently?

FEAR OF SUCCESS

While you may resist change because of fear of failure, you may also resist change out of fear of success. As crazy as it might sound, it's a big stumbling block for many.

Why would this be? Having more freedom, more money, more prestige, a bigger promotion can result in enormous changes in your life—and change is scary. There are also potential losses that come with the territory. Becoming successful might result in potential restrictions, responsibilities and changes.

Here are some examples of how success might seem scary and the fear keeps us self-caged.

More Money

More money is great. Who doesn't want to be a millionaire? But what if it means that you will make more money than your spouse does and this could cause a rift in your perfect relationship? What if it means that people will be coming to you for loans and should you turn them away? Making more money will also likely mean more responsibilities and hours clocked in. Money also brings more haters. Like Biggie said, "More money, more problems." So, as you see, money can also have a down side.

Time

Success may mean less time to relax, hang out with friends, study, exercise, and time with your family, and even sleep.

Or you might get a new job in a higher position but you have to move. Or you get bumped up to being the starter or a captain on your sports team and everybody relies on you.

More Recognition

The more money you make, the more recognition. But this can also put more pressure on you to have to produce. Feeling the need to be your best, you might try to give 100% all the time and this can be stressful.

And this now takes us to the fear of not being perfect.

FEAR OF CHANGE

Change is scary. Not only because of what might happen in our lives if we succeed, but because change brings about instability and unpredictability. The adversity you know is better than the one you don't know, as the saying goes. For this reason, many people don't like to rock the boat and feel it's easier to stay where they are than take the chance of jumping from the frying pan into the fire, or the cage onto the floor.

While it's good to be cautious, too much caution is limiting. As I said previously, you have to "feel the heat." If you don't, by venturing out of your comfort zone, you will stay stuck in the same place. "Insanity," said Einstein, "is doing the same thing over and over again and expecting different results."

How can you overcome a fear of change? Recognize that you fear change and develop strategies to work around it. Think of people you know who dared to venture out and try something new—and how their life changed for the better as a result.

Elon Musk went from getting bullied in school to becoming a successful entrepreneur and CEO of two major science-fiction-type companies—and on the way, almost went completely broke.

At 18, he left South Africa, where he was born, to go to Stanford University to study for his Ph.D.

But after only two days in California, he took a huge risk and left to test his luck in the dot-com boom. He never did return to Stanford or get his Ph.D. And the rest is history.

Mark Zuckerberg dropped out of Harvard and left for California to work on creating Facebook.

Who knows? Maybe you too could overcome your fear of change and take a huge risk that would change the world.

As a start, write down what changes you want to make in your life. Then put this list aside, and when we talk about goals in chapter 9, you'll revisit it

FEAR OF NOT BEING PERFECT

"Perfectionism is not a quest for the best. It is a pursuit of the worst in ourselves, the part that tells us that nothing we do will ever be good enough—that we should try again."
~ Julia Cameron

Along with fear of failure, perfectionism is a very big cage for many people. It involves setting standards that are so high that they either cannot be met, or are only met with great difficulty. We come to think that anything short of being the perfect little boy/girl, student, athlete, husband/wife, career man/woman is unthinkable and that even minor imperfections will lead to catastrophe.

Are you a perfectionist? You are if many of these attributes below describe you.

1. - Often feeling frustrated, depressed, anxious, or angry while trying to meet your standards.
2. - Standards get in the way so you can't meet deadlines or finish a task.
3. - Tendency to beat yourself up for not doing a good enough job after spending considerable time and effort on a task.
4. - Suffering from perfectionist thinking.
5. - Black-and-white thinking: "If I'm not perfect, I'm a failure."
   a. - Catastrophic thinking: "I blurted out the wrong numbers in front of my coworkers and I'll never survive the humiliation."

b. - Overestimating probability: "Although I spent all night preparing for a presentation, I know I screwed up."

c. -"Should" statements: "I never should have asked my boss for a raise."

d. - Chronic procrastination, difficulty completing tasks, giving up at the drop of a hat.

e. - Overly thorough in tasks—spending 4 hours on a task that others spent 30 minutes to complete.

f. - Extreme checking–repeatedly checking for possible mistakes when you've established there are none.

g. - Obsessing over small details like what restaurant to go to.

If this sounds like you, you can overcome your perfectionism and break out of the cage.

OVERCOMING PERFECTIONISM

Step 1: Change Perfectionist Thinking

Think realistically

Replace self-critical or perfectionist thoughts with more realistic and helpful statements.

Here are some examples:

"Nobody is perfect!"

"Everyone makes mistakes."

"All I can do is my best!"

"Not everyone has to like me."

View the world from the other's perspective

If you're a perfectionist, there's a good chance you have a hard time seeing things from another person's point of view. In other words, you tend not to think about how others might see a situation. For example, you might think that you are stupid because you are slow in learning new software.

But your friend might think you are smart, because you persist even though it's difficult for you. Or if you think you are lazy, try to imagine how a close friend might view you or how someone looking up to you might view you.

Learning to view situations as other people might see them can help you focus less on your need to be perfect.

Give yourself a break. It's okay to have a slip of the tongue or gobble up that cookie. You are only human, after all.

Step 2: Stop engaging in excessive behaviors that lead to perfectionism

This is tough to do, but you need to become aware and make every effort to change these behaviors. Here are some thoughts.

Talk at a meeting without first rehearsing what you are going to say in your head. You'll be surprised how well it might turn out.

Don't expect to immediately feel comfortable with the notion of making minor mistakes. You will need to practice and practice.

Don't be discouraged if your anxiety doesn't reduce itself immediately. Keep trying and repeating the exposure as frequently as you can.

Step 3: Overcome Procrastination

Perfectionists tend to be classic procrastinators. This is because they fear making mistakes and so they put things off. "If I can't do it perfectly, I won't do it at all."

Of course, procrastination never works. Eventually, you have to take the test and write the paper, pay the bill, making procrastination only a temporary solution that ultimately increases anxiety.

But you can overcome procrastination. Here are some ways:

Create realistic schedules

Break down larger tasks into more manageable steps. This will make lowering your standards so you don't procrastinate more manageable.

On a chart or calendar, write down the goal or deadline and work towards it, setting small goals along the way.

Remember to reward yourself for each goal you reach.Decide how much time you will spend on a task. Try to view the goal as completing the task, not making it perfect. For more information on how to set realistic and doable goals, see chapter 9 on setting goals.

Set Priorities

As a perfectionist, you are likely to find it hard to decide where you should devote your energy and effort. Prioritize your tasks by deciding which are the most important to accomplish and which are less important. And remember, not every task requires 100%!

FEAR OF REJECTION

No one likes to be thrown out of the tribe, so to speak. We all require the acceptance and acknowledgement of others to feel good. As such, rejection is touchy for everyone.

It is not avoidable, either. Even the brightest, most beautiful/handsome, best athletes, CEO's and most able people on the planet get rejected. It's a fact of life. At some time, we are going to be slighted, turned down for a job, not get into the college of our choice and, of course, the worst of all rejection, failing in our love life. This is all normal.

Walt Disney, a name that needs no introduction, got fired as a youngin' by the editor of a newspaper for lacking in ideas. He started his first cartoon production company from his home and then went bankrupt. Today The Walt Disney Company makes an average revenue of $30 billion dollars annually.

And, of course, everyone knows about Steve Jobs who, at 30-years-old was essentially fired as the CEO of Apple, Inc. after a power struggle with Apple's board of directors. How did Jobs feel about this? Here are his comments at Stanford's 2005 commencement address. "I didn't see it then, but it turned out that getting fired from Apple was the best thing that could have ever happened to me. The heaviness of being successful was replaced by the lightness of being a beginner again, less sure about everything. It freed me to enter one of the most creative periods of my life."

Why Rejection Is So Painful

Though these stories are inspiring, it doesn't negate the fact that rejection is painful. It is especially so if you have low self-esteem, as I did as a kid, and with it a desperate need to please people so they will like and accept you. Any rejection can tear you to pieces and, unknowingly, you may self-cage.

For instance, you may lash out at others before they get the chance to reject you. You may skip a job interview, convinced they will reject you. The list goes on.

Moving On

How can you get past the fear of rejection? You need to build self-confidence and break out of your cages.

And you need to accept that rejection is a part of the risk of living, and to grow means stepping out of your comfort zone even if you get slapped in the face as a result.

You also need to try and not take rejection personally, but instead, view it as a flaw in the other person. Rejection is the other's loss and not your own.

SUMMING UP

Our fears keep us caged. To break out and fly free, we have to overcome our fears.

Some fears are physical, like my fear of flying. But most of the fears that cage us are mental.

They include the fear of:

- *failure*

- *success*

- *change*

- *being perfect*

- *rejection*

Chapter 9 - Decide Your Goals

"If you want to be happy, set a goal that commands your thoughts, liberates your energy, and inspires your hopes."

~Andrew Carnegie

In life, you can wish to break free from your cages all you want, but you are unlikely to do anything without first setting goals to achieve all you desire.

You may wish to play college football, but simply wanting it won't make it happen. You need well-defined steps to reach your goal. For instance, you need to know which colleges offer football scholarships. What grade point average must you have to apply? When do you have to apply by? And so on.

As you can see, setting your goals involves a bit of work in figuring out the steps needed to accomplish them.

STRATEGY 1: SET SMART GOALS

Most everyone who talks about setting goals recommends that you always start with setting SMART goals to make sure your goals are clear and reachable.

SMART stands for:

-Specific   -Achievable   -Time-bound

-Measurable   -Relevant

Set Specific Goals

"A journey of *a thousand miles begins with a single step.*"
~Lao-tzu, Chinese philosopher

Write out your goals in specific detail. If you don't make your goals specific and clear, you will find it hard to focus your efforts and to get charged up to achieve them.

Saying that you want to be a millionaire ain't going to make it happen unless you state specifically how you will achieve this. "Put $100 in savings account this week" is a better goal than just writing down "Put some money in savings." It provides a clear idea of what success will look like and what direction to take.

Specific Actions

Next, outline specific actions you will take to reach your goal. "I will buy a used BMW instead of a new one and put the difference in my savings account." This leaves no doubt about what you need to do to reach your goal of becoming a millionaire.

To aid you in making your goals specific, ask yourself these questions:

Why: What are your specific reasons for accomplishing the goal?

What: What do you want to accomplish? What are the requirements? What are possible pitfalls? What are some alternative ways of achieving the same goal?

How: How will you go about doing what you need to do to accomplish your goal?

When: What time frame should you set?

Where: Where is the best place to live and work to meet your goal?

With whom: Who should be involved?

Set Measurable Goals

To track your progress and stay motivated, goals should be measurable. Include precise amounts, dates, and so on. This will make it easy for you to measure your degree of success. If you define your goal only as "To reduce expenses," you won't have a measure of when you've succeeded. As a result, you will miss out on the satisfaction that comes with knowing you have achieved something.

Ask questions such as:

-*How much?*

-*How many?*

-*What will indicate that I've reached my goal?*

-*How long?*

TIP: Always start a goal with an action verb, like "write," "finish," or "call," versus inactive to-be verbs like "am," "be," "have," and so forth. For example, "Write a daily blog," is far more powerful than, "Be more conscious about blogging often."

Set Attainable Goals

Set realistic yet *challenging* goals. In other words, reach for the sky – but not so high that it's impossible to achieve your goals. If you wish to play for the Lakers, but have not distinguished yourself as a basketball player, you're sure to fail. And you know what this means. You won't break free from your cage of poor self-confidence and you will feel demoralized.

So shoot for flying free to the moon by choosing a goal that is challenging and one that you have to work hard to reach, but is within your grasp

Also, be careful about setting goals when someone or something else has power over you. For instance, getting a promotion depends on who else is up for a promotion. In contrast, setting a goal to get the experience you need to become a top-notch salesman is entirely up to you.

Set Relevant Goals

Be sure your goals are in line with the direction you want your life and career to take. If you wish to start your own software company, make certain this goal accords with your talents, skills and desires.

To find out if your goal is relevant, ask yourself these questions:

-Does it seem worthwhile?	*-Is this the right time?*	*-Does it match my efforts and needs?*

For instance, you might want to gain the skills necessary to become head of distribution within your organization, but is this the right time to undertake the required training and is it a match with your qualifications?

Set Time-Bound Goals

Goals cannot be open ended. They must have a set deadline. And it must be something that you can start NOW.

If you wish to be a millionaire, create a goal to make a million dollars within the next ten years – starting now!

Along the way, you can evaluate how far you've gotten and what new strategies, or even a different direction, might be necessary.

Strategy 2: Set Heartfelt Goals

Set goals that fire you up and have great value and meaning for you. Remember, you were put on this earth for a purpose. Your goals should meet this desire. Once you're charged up, you'll break free from any cage holding you captive.

Strategy 3: Set Goals for the Greater Good

Set goals that will benefit others. Wanting to create a new type of plastic bag that will hold double the amount of groceries at the supermarket might make you good money, but it will further destroy the environment and the future of your children on this earth.

Your message, product, service, art and so forth should be something for the greater good of mankind and the environment. If not, even if you break out of your cage, you will feel deficient and, even, unaccomplished.

Strategy 4: Prioritize Goals

You may have many goals and this is good, but you need to focus and act on those that have the most priority. If you are female, you need to decide if you wish to have a family first and then pursue a career, or have your career first and then devote yourself to your family. If you are male, you need to decide if you wish to start a family and focus on making enough money to support them as I did, or first pursue your dream.

Strategy 5: Be Optimistic

When setting a goal, remember the law of attraction: *Positivity attracts positivity; negativity attracts negativity.*

So focus on what you *will* do rather than on what you *won't* do.

Strategy 6: Break Down Goals into Manageable Tasks

Tip 1: Set Short and Long-Term Goals

Divide your goals into short-term goals; for example, improving your blocking—and long-term goals; for example, getting your MBA.

Tip 2: Break Down Your Goals by Categories

Set goals that cover all areas of your life in which you wish to break out of your cage, grow and evolve.

-Foundation   *-Family*   *-Exercise*

-Faith   *-Mindset*   *-Career*

Take each and jot down five short and five long-term goals that you want to accomplish. For short-term goals, think about what you can manage in the next couple of months. For long-term goals, think about what you want to accomplish over the next three to five years.

_____

_____

_____

_____

_____

Tip 3: Start Small

Remember turtle mode and think baby steps, not grand leaps. Never forget that every journey starts with that first step.

Choose one thing to improve on every day, like replacing apple pie with an apple to meet your goal of eating healthier. Eating fruit like an apple, a banana, or a cup of berries is something most can commit to do consistently and succeed at. Succeeding at this small step will give you the confidence and motivation to take a bigger leap, like giving up sodas in favor of water.

Strategy 7: Use Reinforcement Tools

Tip 1: Make Your Goals Visible

To remind yourself every day of what it is you intend to do, post your goals in visible places: walls, desk, computer monitor, bathroom mirror or refrigerator.

Strategy 8: Visualize Goals

"Imagination's everything.
It is the preview of life's coming attractions."
~Albert Einstein

Imagine being successful, imagine winning that championship, getting that degree or those new shoes. What happened? You felt it? Many of you will have.

Visualization has a powerful effect on the mind. This happens because the brain does not distinguish between an activity visualized and one actually performed. This means that visualizing goals in your head holds as much weight as practicing with your body. If you imagine lifting heavy weights, you will feel physically exhausted afterwards.

Why would this be? The action and the *imagined* action activate many of the same neural networks.

For this reason, virtually all top performers—from athletes to surgeons, to musicians to actors, to business executives— perform the action in their minds before doing it in reality.

Here are some examples:

- *Basketball legend Michael Jordan always pictured the last shot in his mind before he shot a bucket.*

- *Boxing legend Muhammad Ali pictured himself victorious long before the actual boxing match.*

- *Olympic Athlete Jeremy Dodson pictured himself running in the Olympics four years prior to the race.*

Take the time to use the power of your creative mind to create vivid images of your goal.

HOW TO VISUALIZE

Lesson 1: Get detailed

To increase the likelihood of the big picture, see images in great detail.

Lesson 2: Imagine every step

Imagine every step. People who imagine each step are more likely to make it happen.

Lesson 3: Use all the senses

Use all five senses. What are you hearing? Smelling? Touching? Imagine your emotions and bodily sensations when you have achieved the goal. For example, if you want a really nice car... imagine yourself actually driving it, the smooth sound of the engine. Imagine touching it, the shiny lacquer finish, imagine inhaling that new-car smell. Nothing like it! This is a real vision not a hallucination.

Lesson 4: Focus on the positive

See your images with the cup half full, not half empty. Picture yourself as if you have already accomplished your goals. If you wish to lose 20 pounds, see yourself lean in shorts, not downing yourself. If you wish to become a CEO of a big company, see yourself sitting at the head of a long conference table, not slumped in the corner staring at your boss who's lecturing on productivity. If your desire is to visit India, see yourself standing in front of the Taj Mahal.

Lesson 5: Visualize Daily

Ideally, shoot for 10 to 15 minutes a day of visualizing yourself achieving your goal. Remember, you need to do this for 21 days for it to become routine and part of self-leadership.

SUMMING UP

You can't just think that you want to break free from your cage, you have to set goals on how you are going to do this.

Chapter 10: Walk the Walk

Organize/Plan

Life today is more hectic than ever. There never seem to be enough hours in the day to get everything done on your to-do list. At the same time, many of us find that we spend more time on little things than on the important work in our lives and don't leave enough time for pleasure and relaxation. At night, we get into bed stressed and exhausted.

But you can better manage your life by learning how to manage your time, rather than have your time manage you. It's not hard to do.

Just organize your day into manageable, focused blocks of time that include carefully scheduled healthy meal breaks and exercise. Unclutter your life, prioritize and delegate. Once you have your plan in place, stick to it.

Don't Wait and Put in the Effort

I had a friend name K.T., who was caged with the door wide open. He was the poster boy for self-caging. I understand nobody is perfect, but he was just lazy and had opportunities that he didn't take advantage of.

He liked the cage, much like the lion at the zoo, as my coach told me, "Had his food made for him so he didn't have to hunt." K.T. had his maid who did everything for him, just like the lion.

Many times he did break out of the cage but seemed to just want to go back. He was living in a cage with the door wide open. He did/doesn't want to leave.

Nothing in life is free. You have to work for everything that you get; it doesn't come to you. If you sit around and wait for the opportunity to come, you may sit in your cage forever.

If a door shuts, you can't just give up. You have to try another door.

As we've mentioned, expect failures and setbacks. You can't control everything that happens in your life—what your friends do or what your family does, for instance. But you can control your own actions and the effort you give. The prizes you win in life don't come by sitting around and having other people serve you, but by going out and winning them yourself.

Putting It All Together

No matter what you do in life, appreciate the journey, not just the destination. I hope you feel encouraged to get out of whatever has caged you. I understand it's not easy; life is full of cages and we can't stop that. We are all either going into cages, going through cages or coming out of a cage. It's inevitable.

But the problem isn't the cage; the problem is your *attitude* about the cage. Whether a cage makes you or breaks you, whether it defeats you or defines you... It is all up to you!

You don't have to dive into it head first. Remember my turtle philosophy – slow, steady and persistent wins the race. Think gradual change and running your race. This doesn't mean stay still. The amazing realtor Piper Billups said, "Good things come to those who execute." So go and execute!

Remember, every journey begins with the first step, and small successes build upon one another to create momentum. You define your own success! Break out!

Be prepared for a long but fulfilling journey toward breaking free from your cage. Set a long-term plan, monitor your progress and remain open to revising the plan if you aren't getting the results you want.

Let go of what limits you!

#Mode

<u>Acknowledgments</u>

There are so many people who have impacted my life. I wanted to shout out a few people who helped me with this project.

To my parents, my family, Friends and Loved ones: the ones who have had an impact on my life, I thank you and I'm grateful to have you in my life. You all have inspired me. I love you all.

Eric Bieniemy: Thank you for seeing greatness in me when I didn't see it in myself. Thank you for inspiring this book. Thank you for mentoring me, teaching me about life, fatherhood and helping me become a better man beyond the game of football.

Rodney Billups: You've always looked out for CJ and me since Day One and you've cultivated our potential. I can't thank you enough for the amazing impact that you've had on us. Especially me. Thank you for always keeping it real and showing us what's possible.

Mark Littlejohn: You're family, but I wanted to personally thank you for everything you do, cousin. You never get any recognition. You have broken out of many cages and set an example for us. I'm proud of the man and father you've become. You're a true inspiration. .

Jasmine Elizabeth: This wouldn't be possible without you! Thank you for helping me and guiding me. Thank you for supporting me in the pursuit of this project. Thank you for "Return to the Knew." Your book was amazing and it set the tone. It inspired me to write this book. Thank you for showing me it's possible to be an author. Thank you for your continuous support.

Jeremiah "Flip" Benjamin: Thank you for everything you do for the community and the kids out there in California and the world. I appreciate you stepping in and helping me. You are a huge part of why this book is prosperous. Thank you for constantly showing and teaching me new things. Thank you for showing the world and our culture new ways to succeed.

Darian Hagan: Thank you for giving me an opportunity when nobody else would and believing in me. I've watched you break out of many cages and overcome hardship. I'm proud of you!

Michael Pitre: I appreciate you encouraging me to finish this book. Always keep it real with the world and me. I'm proud of you!

To The University of Colorado Boulder: Thank you for seeing me as more than a student and giving me a chance that no other colleges would. Thank you for helping me grow.

Wo: Proud of you bro, keep breaking out of them cages and leveling up. Thank you for pushing me. (Zach, BB, Caleb, CJ, Quila Chris, Big L, Jenks, Ty).LLVJ

Enoch: I remember us talking about this and now it's here, bro. Tough times don't last – tough people do!

Kristen James: Thank you for your support during this process and helping me during my tough times at K-State, you Momma J and the family I love yall.

Julio Flores: Thank you for all you do, You're a huge part of why these pages were brought to life.

Nancy Hutchins: Thank you for proofreading and helping editing this book with me. Thank you for your willingness to help me. You're amazing!

Aunt Nina: Thank you for lending support throughout this process!

Made in the USA
Columbia, SC
12 February 2020

87751859R00089